Strin

Clive Gresswell

erbacce-press publications Liverpool UK 2021
erbacce-press.co.uk

ISBN: 978-1-912455-22-5

Acknowledgements:

Thanks to *BlazeVox* where four of the prose poems in *Strings* were originally published.

Dedication:

...to the poets of Writers Forum (New Series)
where these poems were first workshopped.

Contents:

Poetics for *Strings*.

When writing *Strings* I was looking to find a point where I could build more psychologically-based imagery into my poetry. The immediate aim was to try and replicate, at least to some extent, those quick-flashing images which come into our minds – fleetingly – perhaps for only a fraction of a second. The pieces generally, freeform as they are, unadorned by grammar or punctuation, are meant to delve into this world where the unconscious joins the conscious in the act of setting something new and original down in writing. To delve deeper than some other poetry does.

My influences ranged from Samuel Beckett to the once popular widely-published psychotherapist RD Laing. Its form comes in particular from a book of Laing's called *Knots* that I read sometime in the 1970's. It had small bursts of conversations between a man and a woman who tied themselves up in 'knots' by the way they communicated. This was the form I wanted for my poems complete with the 'knots' one's own thoughts tend to spring on one.

I hope these poems strip down your thinking and leave you nowhere to hide. Catch the naked you inside your animal skin if you will.

Other influences were my reading of Freud and Jung and a range of modern poets from Sean Bonney to Tom Raworth.

I was attempting to try something new to move my poetry forward out of its formal restrictions.

If reading it is akin to an assault on the senses then I am pleased because that is exactly what these poems are supposed to be – particularly when read aloud and in a fast and furious way.

Clive Gresswell July 2021

<u>Strings</u>

hot and melting. that's the trick. i could have waited. walked in on them. the slings and arrows of all that fall. the one in blue blew me a kiss and then to the side crawling with some dismay. magic then. in the fitful eyes that recognize. the black and white newsreel the pinprick on my soul. the very first time i gazed at you and slid into my own skin here we go having told another adventure another flag waving seizure and we will all crumble at once as we take a turn along the esplanade and writing out our holiday memories hot and melting there is always the point of view of the top dog. it might be ian it might be tim or vladimir we can only hope he is satisfied with that and does not want to chase us willy-nilly across the countryside or if our shadows collide with the efforts we made at first. hot and melting. crash and burn to follow the tunnel as it twists and turns inside and out. a shadow of a man.

small and round and perfectly formed no hint of the corners. not here in another place. determined to file through the ashen faced and those who learned with me. what did we learn what is it like to grow some common blood rushing through our ears and inviting us to understand anew. what is in his stillness the inside raw on the outside. well no matter. walk from place to place and along the path where golden love shone say one summer in the city before the lockdown into the water those who were baptized escape the bitter winds moving towards some sort of harmony. and eat. we'll eat and digest and drink ourselves insensible goodbye i go now to the earth. all flesh and then opening my inner eye what you might call my soul. determined to file through.

i and i in submission to your shadow and the ink of ego it traced deep and deeper and then there was time to elongate and twist to snap the emerging synapse from a to b and little routes inbetween lost with you on the holiday of imagination trying to reach my vaster self and i said and i said straight on neither left nor right but buried up to my neck in the holy shit of it those who did not conform and yet i know there are such things as butterflies and even means yes we will go there naked and unafraid but just for now there is this bloody path on which i slip and i recall it was me at two took the thorns and laid them at a strangers door then knocked back the ectoplasmic dream and the fiery sensation.

away. with your running. the figure hauled in circular motions. what is it i tell you. the lash. open your eyes for the lash. what film is it made of. we walked along separate in the circular. speak to me of love said the hog. its hairy ugly face grimacing at the children. the point is the point is he would not choose which in that none of them were perfect his swollen feet were not perfect they came from a poorer time when the children were hauled in circular motion and gyrated like pigs. at the sweet shop. where the policeman came out running and we did not move beyond the wall because of the fear of our own breath and the shadow of the dog who slunk past the dirty outskirts of our dreams.

and the fleet-foot troubles the stones as we walk and bringing into

sharp focus the curse from when we were young so very young and

yet i recall from the outside the mighty roar of the lion and equal of

the lion tamer and fast down the hills 1, 2, 3 in the morning to crow

and coax at all the others whose eyes sit stubborn on the plain and

dipping my toes and mush of the iniquity i say in my own way i

have just as right as left or right or straight on as any other but ma

and da shackle me in and patrol the perimeters of this prison night

and day although i can sometimes mollify them with a sly and

dangerous wink and say i am more than this my foot rotting in my

cakehole expired and i aspire into bring but my being is betrayed

by its very nature. two steps forward and one back & back into

the darkness the flame of my being extinguished for want of some

light.

crawling into. the mush of inevitability where i drew ego and whispered the fleeting id of my desire we all crawl into dressed in the flesh of my nightmares or the sister a shadow towards the light but then crawling into the darkness of inevitability we spoke yes and no wound at the cellular level and where we fell into the mud pushed by ma and da not nourished with movement to come but spat out immediately into the husk of an afterlife the trials and tribulations of those forever flogged me finishing the practice and growing among the way from a to b across skies that make no sense the whirring of the dog curse carried in my arms and crawling into to say reinforce the inevitability of the hung drunk molecule and the writhing of the extras who slip and slide across your vision and the bloody stranger welcomes you in into your own torn gypsy heart. fed on the rebel the stinking stoat and now you no longer move in any circles. your flailing arms and legs fail you. creatures torn from this solitary lagoon fail you.

and he walked on doubled with the pain of it his rattling cry glum glum glum in need of some light conversation but not to free now to be punished by the taller ones the holy ones whose pock-marked faces he had banished from the semi-circle the tiny tread at base one and base two as if he could ever overcome the delicious misdoings the folly of dealing himself with other people's darkness. quite. and all caught out there in the swamp of his being from where he came ra, ra. everything buried up in the hilt. no breath. nothing circular.

walking in the blazing heat there is no respite from this idiotic condition the water and the lice i said to you give me a snatch of memory as we were when the lice did not bother us before the creatures that became known as family who join everyone in the semi-circle whispering pull us on push us on and into the light glowing at the end of night's promise and when i slid on my haunches looking for the magnificent respite and the jewel of a lark throttles the curse say as you did. i cut and i cut to the abominable core and the said things which pass between us neither left nor right. obscuring the brightness of the sun and holding on to whatever morsels they see fit to offer or should i say give with no shame involved and an ample play on the light step which the instructor urges me from time to time from time to time to frequent but with no notion of consequence. just a jig to the left and then to the right with nothing to chase except aspects of me drowning in the drift of my own thoughts. circular day and night. rapid fire worn down to the bone.

softly warm and comfortably distinctly along the dance the path from a to b no custom to share this piggyback hobby somewhere mother there were limits away from the history in the eye of the plague and father said no in the eye of the beholder and your mother was a beauty before and before again all i can offer you at this late stage dancing the light fantastic from a to b where first of all was the number and it was i then further on past the dustbins of insanity a new thought shining because new say see if it is useful to you or not just the same old bind the same old blind alley. it's what i see/what i always saw in the mirror the angry father curses me and says rise up, rise up and face me like a man tomorrow perhaps today i am too busy gazing at nowhere in particular.

the gentle. pulled some sort of vacant stare. a hobby of some sort
if you elongated me and perhaps we would say a or b or run what
i do remember is the place where i was born. bald and crying and
now the bones cut to the quick with the just borrow me this or
lend me that. a time when meaning was black or white and the
playing fields were green and there was always my mutual and
fair friend dolly the corn-doll and though i stared deeply i never
said more on any subject than hello and yet they thrashed me in
the yard and warned me to be more civil. i was elongated after a
fashion cut my hair and beard and went as far as the stink farm.
but who really is there left to apologize to. mark out the sores. the
bleeding prayers. hollow ghosts crawl along the page as my eye
slips to the suffering. it takes. hollow stares hollow darkness of the
night. hush i am cold. later i will be warm. that will be the blessed
time to crack open i wonder if left or right is the right i mean the
correct way to proceed. where is the ambush tonight. will it make
any clearer sense.

halt. stretch. and smell the scent of the battlefield. you could have said the army marched. you could have said. yes. or no. now i am too weary and infirm. filling in the endless forms. which way. left or right or perhaps still straight on. for what purpose do i dissect this monologue. is it true it could be anymore pleasing to me than a more or less.halt.stretch and sniff for the direction. like some near formed brother who hastens to plot my shadow the very marrow of me. sucked and exploited to merit what? inches? quiet now as the sun the son dressed in the rags. and ambition? what of its shadow. its dreamy spires. halt. stretch. i am not liquid. not rushing headlong out of the tap... i am passed filling out the endless forms. none of them have ever held any meaning. no, it has always been her and her alone. and alone. i dabble in society. my feet tire. i am weary and would but rest. singing softly to myself with the mouth that knew you and then danced and then danced.

time the manacle of i his dead weary feet turning in haste to
question once he saw with his own his own bloodshot eyes the
manacle the dead weary feet in protest always marching in protest
never i support i support something inside breaks every ambition
and then the fall tempered in the bloody ink of his/her exposition
and the crybaby rank of ma and pa as they threw whatsisname i
never knew into the river on his lifelong course reciting which
came first the nihilism or the poetry or the reading he had expelled
the tossed creature blank into the moonlight and the howling of
wolves could he give them a name say ma and pa and he climbed
the mountain jagged and bleeding with the twisted word from his
tongue stammering in awe.

darkness. towards the light. screams. halt who goes there sliding on his filthy stomach. neither left or right. a semi-circle. dark eyes. up to the ceiling. we will follow in his stupor. drunkenness time and time again. where was the privilege? all white and done up in your furs. certainly not. screams. i will follow you along the road. pay for my twitching misdemeanour. listen again to the great roar of a warning. tap-tap-tapping down the road. his legs felt weak. his praying legs. shot now where he had first seen da. sorry to have tripped over you disease. he says to the others on stage he cannot go on. the race is not always to the swift. turn left right go centrally. turn in a circle. not to confuse those who always end up on the corner. blood on his lip. like it was on that first day of prayer when he limped home across the square. maybe not him exactly .or another. or perhaps some quick-bleeding shadow. of a tooth.

so cold. i told you it would be like this. the shame is from there

there is no turning. this way or that. cold and warm all the same

ma and pa with the poison you inject into my food. at one time

just to know you would have been enough. but now ma and pa it's

all too twisted my idea of you and how i was and i wonder what

that has got to do with love. just the final act. so cold. and dark.

but from there there is no turning. the deeds have been done and

the die has been cast. we could try and walk it off. mumbling. but

where would that lead us. in the cold and dark and no guide from

the times we tried before then about all i could manage to have

said was hello and then a little bit later well goodbye. you cannot

say i didn't try ma when all the chips were down. i tried and failed.

it leaves a scar ripped from the umbilical. deep down drowning in

the emotion of any event feared on the journey the journey from

me to you and back.

we walk say as police informants say with our hobnail boots deep

in our mouths and we walk the strange estates in pairs where first

the adverb tore at my gypsy throat and i sang loud and clear into

the air a song of love but only of the foolishness of humanity.

pah at times it leads you to despair the cold truth of each man

for himself and i cried the night my brother died in the arms that

could hold him no longer in peace in the one and only true peace

and as his chattering to the wind stopped and he cried there is no

more hope as i filmed him then we stepped into the circle and sat

staring at the stars and as i sang out my eyes began to weary and

they would have shut but for the harlot who was herself singing a

lonely tune from beyond the waves.

floating i and i on the sea or say reaching for the sky and the consequence of which the stammer and then say the shuffle my memory draws breath 1,2,3 causes me to blink and now it shatters in my mind like the dog whose lead escapes me as i turn to run and then the lice force you back into my memory shaking and clucking and once again i heard you laughing slap into my face what a rigmarole a weight off my chest though and now saying as the french do the freedom to love every bit of me even the defiled and those who stroked ma and da and as i walked on along the towpath i fell into the river cursing my luck and i pushed myself ignorant and afraid naked and along the bank tears welled up inside me as i shouted out i am lost i am lost bring me some of your furniture you poets and so they did tables and chairs and we used them for firewood for the wind was bitter and we had as yet no door i asked ma and pa but they were old and weak themselves. crestfallen. the sore on the ankle. the right one. i should ask but i may only forget. the doctors could not agree save to venture that i was 1,2,3 an extreme case of the cold. my bones picked clear by the vultures. rotting in my memory the very nature of abusive greetings. today we do not play so much although i still invoke the missing ma and pa who anyway were never capable of making me complete. like 1,2,3 they tried.

he sucks at the boundary. walled in by the contusion lilting his confusion i said at the light to make myself scarce of the dos and don'ts the intimate pleasure of colliding worlds each of us walled in by the boundaries defined by an illusion and as i chatter into the rawness of my bleeding heart from which the poppy seeds were spilled and as i leapt the boundary i hammered with the froth of my fists the waning of a to b and as the slick arrow of dust engorges his reason and i suck at the boundary since birth and onwards crawling and walking then run apace if that is to be my sequence which i must assume it is without the luxury of picking at untamed thoughts some guard slipped into this mush some guard wrestles for no good reason. hey man it's a job crawling and walking then run apace. no reward.

walking say walking having word spit anger in the frozen husk
the membrane of my first being gentle and mild until the howling
gripped verbs and raw in tooth and claw my shadows betrayed me
with no answer to the where or why of nothing just the drip dripdrip
on the forehead tapping 1,2,3 in the ambulance of societies dreams
the crash of those as i knelt in the stench and the shit and the mud
eyes closing with a sad blink 123 tear for what the garden with
no way through the maze and nothing to take me to the joy of its
centre i stumble around the outside wasting my covid breath ladies
and gentleman and before my eye was ravaged my mouth could
fully engage in laughter. and in kissing another human being but
now gripped verbs grip anger at the circus before the clowns and
they bite into my thorny flesh the membrane of my thorny flesh
exploded in the distance and left shellshock biting into my flesh.

truth outlasts eh and oh as they split the filter 1,2,3 between say id and reason and the subdivision which borders memories of this neuron dying in the rebirth of new experiences on the sense boundary caked in mucus of the old crawling the 1,2,3 heard dying in the wings the bonfire of those who let the fireworks dance and lauded the network of tunnels amid the lords and ladies who declare in absolute terms the flickering and why the neon i tremble at their power and so later when out on patrol i went back for my son eh and oh the dying 1,2,3 and dreams lasted well into the morning and my path was now black on grey as i pulled on the twisted and tortured flesh the searing scars trapped in a vivid decoy the word began.

the belly-laugh. and gurgle up at notion a fixation to notion b and demanding answers from the movement fall headlong into fail the distance say between hark and see a clear blue yonder where the sun shines the majestic magical burst this ego and mission how nice to greet you and swap the journey from a to b and it's no reflection given on you that at the appropriate time i pulled out a verb and swallowing whole the gist of it all i could think was here is a fine day stuck in my craw and no movement left or right and this reminder of my companion shadow who did not speak but wearied at the need to get the permissions for slaughter the same old record spinning round and round and the merchants offering childhood dreams but cut in mid-air and the solitude of collecting them and reciting in the long echo of the corridor the constant battle for freedom won and lost in equal measure.

at first the crawling thru the piss and shit the abc and i said 1,2,3 the amount of ammonia crawling the twinkling of an egg divides and next to sleep i am swallowing the crawling and i parted saying since to offer some semblance of sense the adoring ma and pa oh they surely cannot bring themselves to waste this or that or as a word oh and ho trembles from their lips as they stumble and fumble linking together in a sort of animal chain and wordlessly 1,2,3 delight in their own passion it has nothing to do with my love. i just rest my feet by the boundaries and ponder why this restless nature not that i have ever been beyond the village where a to b were first born in the twinkling of an aspect you can only see thru the telescope and the junk i carry round in my pockets including a handkerchief for dribbling and some shrubs for romantic purposes should a bound over the fence and in the shed mirror see my face and praise be despite what i thought he is a beauty though worn and torn from years of despair and years of disrepair even though he cannot bring himself to say it he dons his hat and moves on to a more fertile neck of the woods. where the images are kinder and the remoteness slides him along his journey. to a value which even in the heat of tonight can be imagined.

plus etc out of the arsehole and conjoining with the mouth he swallowed verbs cast them into the world with no thought none at all for the worn and frayed nature of its journey on this dark night around the village from a to c and he wonders briefly what that means so he can file it in the correct hole in memory or at least name it as an experience once tried and best avoided or failing that to mention its sensation and try again to replicate it perhaps having cut the heart of it out and tied it lovingly or not to the ganglion the husk or his search in dressing gown continues past any sensation remotely startled with a name that human flesh will recognize he thinks of the 1,2,3 of waves never beaten and he bows his head and gasps.

that's your trouble eh ah and heave ho away with ma pa and those lice you carried deep down into wherever you could unburden yourself on the next creature hurrah to feel so much lighter yourself without having lost should one say freedom because of course it might not be that one could most possibly say that going by experience you and the shadow will still be in the village and who's to say you will not happen round again for a second or third time and each time there is a crossing over across the field and down long to the river and the shadow mumbling 1,2,3 will answer the question that burns on your lips the decoy where the question what will you know anymore after they tie you up and dance around you humming and singing and 1,2,3 you blurt out the verbs from your sleep down your throat and away from your confessions fashioned in replication of the deep but it sighs and twists and turns away from the abc boundary ripped from the core of your being and offering no respite.

About the author:

Clive Gresswell is a 3-year-old innovative writer and poet. He has a poetry MA and a BA First Class in Creative Writing both from the University of Bedfordshire where he studied as a mature student.

For 30-plus years before that he worked as a newspaper journalist.

He has written poetry on and off for as long as he can remember and most recently has been published in *BlazeVox, Poetry Wars, Tears In The Fence, aglimpse of, The View From Here, Marble Poetry, Dead Snakes Po mick's Dead Typewriter, Clod Magazine* and many others. He has two other poetry collections both with Knives, Forks and Spoons Press, *Jargon Busters* and *Rages Of The Carbolic.*

Clive is married with two grown children and lives in Bedfordshire.